THE APPASSIONATA POEMS
by David Citino

Cleveland State University Poetry Center

ACKNOWLEDGMENTS

The author wishes to thank the editors of the following periodicals, in which some of these poems first appeared.

"Letter to Sister Mary Appassionata, America's Adviser to the Lovelorn": AKROS.

"Sister Mary Appassionata's Lecture to the Eighth Grade Boys and Girls on the Things of this World, the Things of the Other": THE BELOIT POETRY JOURNAL.

"A Lesson in Anatomy" from "Sister Mary Appassionata Lectures the Pre-Med Class": THE BENNINGTON REVIEW.

"Sister Mary Appassionata Lectures the Creative Writing Class: The Evangelist": CHICAGO REVIEW.

"Sister Mary Appassionata Lectures the Bible Study Class: Noah": DESCANT.

"Sister Mary Appassionata Lectures the History Class: Life of the Saint": THE HOLLINS CRITIC.

"Doctrines of the Breath" from "Sister Mary Appassionata Lectures the Pre-Med Class": THE PLAINS POETRY JOURNAL.

"The Four Fluids" from "Sister Mary Appassionata Lectures the Pre-Med Class": SAN JOSÉ STUDIES.

"Sister Mary Appassionata Lectures the Eighth Grade Boys and Girls: The Second Day" and "Sister Mary Appassionata Lectures the Eighth Grade Boys and Girls on the Nature of Eloquence": SOUTHERN HUMANITIES REVIEW.

"Sister Mary Appassionata Lectures the Creative Writing Class: Life of the Poet; Or, the Storm": SOUTHERN POETRY REVIEW.

"Sister Mary Appassionata Lectures the Creative Writing Class: Naming Everything Again," "Sister Mary Appassionata Lectures the Bible Study Class: Homage to Onan," and "Sister Mary Appassionata Lectures the Clinical Psychology Class on the Life and Death of Blessed Eustochium of Padua": THE SUN: A MAGAZINE OF IDEAS.

"Sister Mary Appassionata Lectures the Eighth Grade Boys and Girls: The Family Jewels": TENDRIL.

"Sister Mary Appassionata Lectures the Folklore Class: Doctrines of the Strawberry": THE TEXAS REVIEW.

"Sister Mary Appassionata Lectures the Home Ec Class: The Feast": WIND/LITERARY JOURNAL.

"Sister Mary Appassionata Lectures the Eighth Grade Boys and Girls on the Life and Death of St. Teresa": THE YALE REVIEW.

With the support of the Ohio Arts Council

for Mildred and John

CONTENTS

THE APPASSIONATA POEMS

SISTER MARY APPASSIONATA LECTURES THE EIGHTH GRADE BOYS AND GIRLS: *EVERY DAY ANOTHER SNAKE*

And God gave Adam hands, fingers
smooth enough to soothe, deft enough
to create, arms long enough to reach,
but Adam sinned by trying to please
himself alone, so God made Eve, and
to her too gave hands, fingers, arms,
but Eve sinned by wanting to please
herself before all else, so God was forced
to make the snake, but by this time
He'd learned a lesson, and made it
limbless, and its slither and hiss
made Adam work, and Eve, until
their hands grew rough as pumice,
fingers gnarled from scrabbling for roots
in rocky soil, sewing greasy skins
callous-tough with blunt bone needles,
arms bent from a winter's weight
of firewood, a spring field's
depth of stone and clay.

Still today women and men come
into the world with the means to soothe,
create and reach, but a burning lust
to please nobody else. Every day
God's forced to make another snake.

SISTER MARY APPASSIONATA LECTURES
THE EIGHTH GRADE BOYS AND GIRLS:
THE SECOND DAY

When He said on that first dark day
"Give me light," there flew in
from nothingness legions of creatures
plumaged in sunshine, each pair of wings
a song. He gave them names like "Basso"
and "Contralto," "Wind-in-Pines" and "Lark."
He spent the rest of the day listening.

But by the piercing dawn of the second day
the song fell apart, harmony wavering
and cracking, the heavens sounding like
a turntable with too many records piled on;
and He didn't care for the way some angels
sang to others, wings fluttering together,
on every cloud an act of brazen love.

So when He divided the waters under
the firmament from the waters above
the angels whose feathers grew dim with sweat,
wet with wanting and coarse enough to touch
could no longer fly, and fell terribly
from the sky, screams fading as they dropped
through air and earth and into fire.

Thus were demons created, numbering,
the Talmud tells us, exactly 7,495,926
though some believe each infant brings along
when he falls to earth another thousand.
This is how things got the way they are.
This second day alone of all the seven
of the week wasn't called "good."

SISTER MARY APPASSIONATA LECTURES THE EIGHTH GRADE BOYS AND GIRLS:
THE FAMILY JEWELS

In the beginning He put man's parts
of love where today you find the nose,
and woman's where her mouth is now.
But she grew too lean and hungry;
he couldn't stop sneezing. Loving,
they couldn't catch their breath.
Neither could get a word in edgewise.

So He put them where today you find
the hands, but it became too hard
to separate the gestures of friends
and lovers. An embrace came to mean
too little, a handshake much too much.
The tribes couldn't discern work from play,
war from peace, itch from scratch. So

He put the instruments of love where
they belong, mouth for ardor, zeal
and pleas, nose for scents, hands
to make or break, give and take, things
of passion closer to the heart than
brain, veiled as all great beauty
must be. Hidden from the greedy

and profane, the family jewels.

SISTER MARY APPASSIONATA LECTURES
THE BIBLE STUDY CLASS: *NOAH*

Months and months adrift
and more marooned on a mountain
in a leaking, three-storied boat of gopher wood
filled with his family,
all clean animals by sevens, unclean
by twos, stench of beasts, mildew and pitch
a powerful perfume wafting to heaven,
incense of all flesh.

The first forty days they hated Him, hearing
beyond bellow and babble below
and rain on the roof loud as static
on a stormy night
the faint cries of those they floated by,
whose only sin was to be born
outside the covenant.
One by one the unbelievers lost their grip
or grew too faint to stroke and kick
and slipped back into the sea
all life once had crawled from,
lungs and fingers a useless evolution.

Then it stopped. Hate became fearing
then vigilance and resolution. It was
the most precious cargo ever to float.
They had to love, and love again.
Hating could only mean another storm.
They were the world compressed to three hundred cubits
by fifty by thirty,
one jagged rock, tree or temple-top
from joining the bloated things
floating toward them and away
white as bone, as salt.

House of all seed, memory and gene,
every last word, there was nothing for them but
to practice being fruitful.

Even the beasts recognized the obligation,
screaming elephants plaiting trunk and tail
into lovers' knots, camels undulating
humps, rocking the boat
with their lumbering enthusiasm,
sparrow, dragonfly and crow,
nighthawk and finch in twos reckless
in air, rabbit, pig, goat and dog
glassy-eyed, love an essence, pulse, hunger,
every male rigid as death
minute by minute, females damp as April dew,
flopping about like trout out of water,
coming together for all they were worth,
dancing over the killing waves.

In those days, not to exceed
their parents' voyaging,
not to last just long enough, was to perish.
Learning to keep afloat
just above danger, like the dove in search of olives,
they taught us generation,
and that endurance always comes in pairs.

SISTER MARY APPASSIONATA LECTURES
THE HUMAN BEHAVIOR CLASS:
ONE MOUTH, LOVE AND ACHE

Because God put in one mouth
both tongue and teeth, each of us
must give and take both love and ache,
wear the masks of song and snarl,
learn how often words are made to break.

SISTER MARY APPASSIONATA LECTURES
THE EIGHTH GRADE BOYS AND GIRLS
ON THE NATURE OF THE CANDLE

There are many instances during the Middle Ages of persons
having a candle made, as a special devotion, of the same
height or the same weight as themselves.
                    —Curiosities of Popular Customs

It stands to reason. Wax crafted by bees,
tallow of vegetable or beast rendered just hard enough
to stand, to support the flame that dances
dangerously before the slightest breath, wick
running the body's length, spinal cord
that makes all parts a whole, intelligence
warming whatever comes near, touch of love,
to dispel the sentence of night after night,
only need to be, but eating a hole
in the center, faith consuming flesh from the inside,
running toward the heart, a fuse,
utter dark biding its time under the tongue,
inside each tooth and bone, life drowning
in the rising tide of life, deadly depth
of every day, price we're made to pay
for our season of light, last breath
a hiss or sigh as sun floods windows
to bear the soul away, what's left of us lying
gutted, guttered, cold, scents
of our brief wisdom lingering in the room.

SISTER MARY APPASSIONATA LECTURES
THE SCIENCE CLASS:
FOSSILS, PHYSICS, APPLE, HEART

Fossil bones, splintered bits of pelvis,
jawbone, tooth and skull aren't
of early apes and men
but of fallen angels made by greed too gross
to fly, who shattered when they hit the ground.

We know from physics every clock
winds down, each woman and man lies down
one more time than necessary for sleep or love.
Every movement culminates in stone,
each light and life in the ocean of night.

Drowned bodies, drunkards, heroes, saviors
surface always on the third day.

Virgin wool cures the deepest ache or burn.

Girls with big breasts and too much heart won't
fit into heaven. The boy who can unclasp
a girl's brassiere with one hand
knows too much for his own good
and all his life will have his hands full,
his mouth open at the wrong time.

The key to happiness? Knowing every second
of every day what to do with the hands,
when to loose or hold the tongue.

The holiest creatures are those that fly. God
Himself's part falcon, cuckoo, pelican, dove.

The girl who indulges herself
by climbing spiked fences, riding a horse
with too much passion, stooping too often
to pick mushroom or orchid

or dreaming of lovers who feel as she does
will from the wedding night on
be too easy on her husband.

Man's the only animal dumb enough to try
to cry back the dead, take
another's life only out of spite,
give his life for love.

Those whose eyebrows meet can never be trusted.

Women named Agnes always go mad.

No hunger justifies eating an apple
without first bringing it to life by breathing
on it, filling it with beauty
by rubbing it across the heart.

SISTER MARY APPASSIONATA LECTURES THE SEX EDUCATION CLASS: *DOCTRINES OF THE KISS*

Behold the birds of the air, how
they bill and coo, the nuzzling
of beasts in each field, elephants
even, braiding lumbering trunks.
Observe cats licking kittens, dogs
how they sniff, baboons groom.

Homer, wise as he was, was blind
when it came time to kiss. Celts
could find no word for it.
Egyptians taught us how to inhale
at one another to unite two souls.
Eskimos, Maoris and Malays press

noses. One Yakut rubs another's
cheek with cold, cold lips, then
waits for inspiration. The French
sin with the tip of the tongue,
grow so hot together they lose
all sense of up or down. Babies

and lovers suckle and bite,
mothers and lovers peck, heal our
every wound. It's the way we set
our seal, make peace, betray
another's savior or mate, bring
ourselves luck, take leave of

our senses, comrades. When we
kiss, every sleeping beauty grows
aroused for dawn, each frog becomes
charming prince. The kiss
makes one of two, involves all ten
senses: savor and feel, love's

scents, whisper and tongue, look;
yet nothing we do, no gesture
makes us more ethereal, gets us
farther from the solitary hell of
bone. When we give our lips away
we're never more ourselves.

SISTER MARY APPASSIONATA LECTURES
THE SEX EDUCATION CLASS:
HISTORIA SEXUALIS

In every drop of semen are seven-times-seventy
angels, golden, man-warm and God-faced, who
use their wings to swim. Each egg
inside a woman bears a portrait of the Virgin.

To see where one so lovely came from, Nero
slit open his mother's belly,
made a shrine of her pelvis.

St. Peter appeared to Agatha in prison
just before she was torn apart
to return to her on a silver plate
the breasts she'd lost the night before
to a Roman and his stubby sword.

Who knows the size of a man's nose
knows the length and circumference of the art
that grows below.

When Adam lost his rib he also lost
the hair that flourished on his palms.

If every act of passion together or alone
didn't cost a year of life
women and men would live forever.
If you move together, as you were made to do,
you must wait for one another. At the instant
of sharpest joy a year of life's exchanged.
If you accept this gift before the one
you're with gets his or hers, you've sinned
the greatest sin and must, the moment strength
returns, begin to move again.

SISTER MARY APPASSIONATA LECTURES
THE EIGHTH GRADE BOYS AND GIRLS
ON THE NATURE OF ELOQUENCE

German tribes hung the heads
of their most eloquent dead
in trees, where, open-mouthed,
they'd sing as long as bone
endured to the rhythms
of God's endless waltz, the wind.

Kleomenes of Sparta kept the head
of his most trusted friend Archonides
in a honey jar, to consult
in times of crisis, for when
things are most bitter
no counsel's sweeter than that
of one who's loved beyond the grave.

The Irish mixed a fistful of brains
from a lost comrade with the earth
he shadowed and made bitter
by his fall, molding a weapon that,
when tempered by the fire and lament
of a long night's vigil, would live
again when flung, finding the murderer
by listening for his voice,
looking into his face, smart enough
to take a shattering revenge,
eloquent enough to shape a song
his sons would sing forever
after he fell back to dust and clay.

SISTER MARY APPASSIONATA LECTURES
THE CINEMATOGRAPHY CLASS:
LATE, LATE MOVIE

During each black and white frame
of *It Came From Beneath the Sea*,
while lovers walk about in twos
or threes, climb stairs together,
lock and bolt their doors,
the ocean moans just behind or below,
hisses slowly up the beach where
they lie entwined, a brackish greed
seething weedy and shrill, a rage.

But the breathless truths of those
who've glimpsed the thing
about to slither and roar through
its rites ashore are thought
too passionate, mad. Waves
conquer the harbor in time. Scene
after scene, each actor becomes
an island. The sea screams to be
heard over rising violins, god

who's come back for his children.

SISTER MARY APPASSIONATA LECTURES
THE CREATIVE WRITING CLASS:
NAMING EVERYTHING AGAIN

. . .and whatsoever Adam called every living creature, that
was the name thereof.

We're designated to travel
from a world where nothing needs
a name to this, where all things cry out
for one. *Cleveland, Ohio.*
Ascension of Our Lord Church.
Giovanni. John. Father.
Eastern Daylight Saving Time.
Undertaker.
Extreme Unction.
Heart.
Beat.
We're made to describe the way
from dark and silence to here,
through every letter, to learn that,
sure as night defines the day, to be
means naming everything again.

SISTER MARY APPASSIONATA LECTURES
THE HOME EC CLASS: *THE FEAST*

On time for every meal
whether I set them a place
or not, the family ghosts
assemble around the table.
My parents and theirs, dead

uncles, cousins and friends
light as steam, subtle as
anise, bay leaf or sage,
study me as I pierce and carve,
slice and chew, pause to savor.

Grease of flesh stains lips
and fingertips, coats teeth
and tongue as rust does iron
or dust the porcelain figurines
in the proper homes of

proper old ladies. Course
after course, meal after meal
and still they're unsatisfied.
Grandfather, speck of oregano
stuck between front teeth,

wipes sauce red as heart's blood
from his plate with a crust,
holds up a glass to ask for
more wine. "But you can't be
thirsty," I whisper. We're

destined to meet like this
three times each day, the family
become a rite, a thirst we'll
never slake, hunger ever
unappeased, our need, the feast.

LETTER TO SISTER MARY APPASSIONATA, AMERICA'S ADVISER TO THE LOVELORN

Q.
My husband's heart's gone
fat and blind, heavy
as a side of beef twisting
slowly in an icy locker,
ham hocks and pork snouts
in the market's cooler, lungs
porous as torn cheesecloth,
two handfuls of greasy suet,
tongue rough as the bull's.

Where love once reared
its proud red head a lamprey
wriggles, limp as old garden hose.
There was a time he could blast
off its silver maple limb
a new brown squirrel
at two hundred yards. Now
he can't see a thing below his
belly. What do you advise?

A.
Every dream disobeyed
becomes by light of dawn
a wound, five pounds more
of ache: lungspot, heartclot,
stone stuck up duct, clogged glands,
chilled glans, handfuls
of vandal cells rioting through
a body's bourgeois avenues.
Heed the dreams, love, you'll

make him over again.
Saved by the all-too-human need
to sleep and dream at the same time,
you'll learn what to wear, where
to have the hole dug, how to
lower him away under stone in a spray
of holy water and tears, cut mums,
poppies, lilies, baby's-breath.
In time all milk turns, meat goes bad.

Soon enough you'll be one again,
sweet and fresh, everlasting. Like death.

SISTER MARY APPASSIONATA LECTURES
THE HISTORY CLASS: *LIFE OF THE SAINT*

All his life it hurt like
ice on a bad tooth to live
in the body: lungs gravel-loud,
throat scalding at each inclination,
bones kindling-brittle when he

misstepped or, trying to cast off
too soon, was yanked back to earth.
The toughening, savage heart arrhythmic,
each silence between beats
a premonition, always too fast or slow

for him to keep in step yet
not once overtaking desire.
The magic wand between the legs,
stately pine or limp garter snake
at the worst of times, its will

his own. He saw at once what
depth and breadth meant to the deer,
the sparrow and calf, the trout,
mouth snapping shut on the hurt
of its last supper. His parents

grew to hardened hearts, bags
of precious wind, bushels of teeth,
hair, bone, guilt and rings. Flesh
a target of every barbed hunger,
one more than it could elude at last,

the weight, darkness he was made to bear.

SISTER MARY APPASSIONATA LECTURES
THE BIBLE STUDY CLASS: *HOMAGE TO ONAN*

Resurrection man, father
of the race and genocide,
puppeteer playing God,

you're empty gesture,
open hand a blessing, fist
a curse. As powerful

nearly as the one who
waits with finger on button
poised to end it all

with the biggest bang.
Impossible as the needle
through the camel's eye,

love born dying at your feet.
What's the sentence to fit
such crime? As part of

your passion, to endure
whenever alone desire's
shivering frictions until

you're worn out, to bear
the unbearable weight,
gravity of humanity, to

stumble down streets
thronged with lovers fit
for one another, those who

didn't fail, to move to death.

SISTER MARY APPASSIONATA LECTURES
THE RELIGION AND MYTHOLOGY CLASSES:
FROGS AND FORESKINS, HEART AND TONGUE

A frog from Egypt's plague, piece of reed
from baby Moses' yacht. Two lumps of lard—
what's left of Lawrence and Joan. A piece
of Shadrach's unsinged robe. Pine shavings
curlicued from Joseph's plane, sawdust
from his rasp, divine chips off
the old block. The Bambino's foreskin.
Feathers from Noah's dove, droppings from
the one that blessed the Apostles' tongues,
the raucous jay Francis shut up with his
simple singing. Feathers from
the engendering wings of Gabriel.
Wormy core of Adam's unswallowable apple.
Comb from the cock that crowed to reproach
Peter. Bones from Balaam's
eloquent ass. Feet of four and twenty crows
knocked out of the sky by Loreto's
high-flying house. Pickled in a canning jar:
Lucy's most discerning eyes, Agatha's nipples,
the herring bone Blaise made the boy cough up,
whole and unaltered hymens of Veronica
and Mary, Holofernes' ear, Cecilia's
vocal cords, heart and tongue of Isaac Jogues,
Abel's skull, irreparably shattered.
A quart of milk from Mary's right breast.

We can't be damned for not believing in these;
only for being so cocksure this world's
a place narrow as the space between our own
eyes and ears, death's-head cell of darkness and bone,
hell of thinking always only that we know.

SISTER MARY APPASSIONATA LECTURES
THE CLINICAL PSYCHOLOGY CLASS
ON THE LIFE AND DEATH OF
BLESSED EUSTOCHIUM OF PADUA

Most of the townsfolk who clumped
each night around the convent wall like
leukocytes around an infection
and demanded that she be shut up for good,
most thought her possessed
of too little morning, too much night.
Daughter of a nun who had no alms
to give a handsome beggar
and no qualms about giving herself instead,
she was always mother's little girl,
confusing give and take, in and out,
love and love. Her pious smiles adorned
the curses she recited each time some demon
slipped between her lips
to waltz and polka her around the floor.
She once was found alone in her cell
naked as Jesus in the manger, eyes
shut tight but smiling the smile
you don't get from dreaming.
The sisters, turning their faces to avoid
the devotion and despair wedded
in her eyes, tried to make her pure again
with the fire of the scourge. How such
holiness hurt her isn't recorded.
After death the embalmers read
with trembling fingers just below the breast
the scarred letters in a child's hand,
J E S U S. She's patroness of those
pulled apart by gravities of earth and sky,
all who're not themselves alone, emblem
of the darknesses that frame each day.

SISTER MARY APPASSIONATA LECTURES
THE CREATIVE WRITING CLASS:
THE EVANGELIST

John, Zebedee's son, best writer
of the twelve, you made Him, then
with a critical eye watched Him
shiver and mope through the final supper,
learned His voice and hate for the state
so well you made them your own,

until years later, head nodding
with the fleeting certainties of age,
you filled a book with sixes and sevens,
locust and scorpion swarming over
sinners who winked at revelation,
giggled at anything you had to say.

Preaching to Rome's Senate
from your cauldron of bubbling oil,
finding yourself unable to die
with so many manuscripts unpublished,
you taught us writing justifies
doubt and loving, showed us

words are always our salvation.

SISTER MARY APPASSIONATA LECTURES
THE THEOLOGY CLASS
ON THE LIFE AND DEATH OF ST. TERESA

She's become a journey.

Her left arm's at Lisbon,
fingers of the right hand at Seville, Avila, Paris,
Brussels, Rome.
Right foot in Rome, a slice of flesh.
One tooth in Venice.
Piacenza boasts of a napkin stained with her blood.
Milan keeps a piece of the heart, another tooth.
Lump of her flesh in Naples, scapular.
Her slippers at Avila,
most of the torso at Alva,
at Cagliari her veil.
The wooden cross she used to beat the demons
sent to try her, at Rome. Also Brussels.
Two very large slices of flesh in Krakow.

She lived to keep herself intact.
At the instant of death love tore her to pieces.

SISTER MARY APPASSIONATA LECTURES THE CREATIVE WRITING CLASS: *LIFE OF THE POET; OR, THE STORM*

She spent that night shivering
the storm away in the enormity
of her bed, hands clenched
between legs, carried away by dream.

He looked like Jesus, face contorted
by passion and thorn. He smelled
of gin. He carried something
like a tree, one end scraping

a furrow in the dusty street.
His sandals slapped the soles
of his feet as he walked. She
followed, two steps to every one

of his, but gained no ground.
A hot wind hit her like a horrible idea.
She swelled at bodice and hip. "My
little girl," he said, but her profile

gave her away. He put something
against her, took her breath away.
So suddenly she was all woman. What
hurt her so when she awoke was that

nothing had changed. Every night
since, she wakes at least once to
the roaring of heartbeats, blood, bed
quaking with thunder, fighting for air

in a room loud with winds of words,
the storm consuming her outside and in.

SISTER MARY APPASSIONATA PROVES TO THE ENTOMOLOGY CLASS THAT WOMAN AND MAN DESCENDED FROM THE CRICKET

Our mother and fathers,
sojourners in bogs, architects
of prairie clods, perennials
strewn over mountainsides,
forders of roiling creeks, herds,
loving under thatch and star,
each word together a bellows
heartening the flame, sang
to summer rain and generation,
feared only the sudden shrill bird
of fire or wind. Where they fell
cities were raised. We lost our ear
to concrete and brick, thick rivers
stagnant under iron spans, tug
and barge contending with siren,
horn, raucous hell of press, mill,
forge. Tonight just beyond
the bedroom wall our parents and the wind
will return to soothe earth's
August fever with a cool hand,
remind us of love's sympathetic magic,
leaping and creaking from clump
and bush, thick weedy field,
chanting the history of the world.

SISTER MARY APPASSIONATA LECTURES
THE THEOLOGY CLASS
ON THE RESOURCEFULNESS OF DEMONS

When it's time for study
they hang on my eyelids,
remind me of Chablis'
sweet French kiss, make the window
a shade too enthralling. They
take up residence under the tongue,
and when I most need to be
an inspiration I'm made
to stutter, hem and haw. One
sits between my legs, and when
I'm in the middle of abstinence
and beauty strides into the room
on muscled thighs, imposing
itself between decades of the rosary,
makes outrageous demands, upsetting
the fragile balance I've
struggled to erect. In the library
they turn pages dark
with the laughter of lark and jay,
tittering of children
in the garden that's summer, bark
and whine of distant dogs. Much as we do,
a demon's what we leave undone. Far
as we go, a demon lies an inch
beyond, taunting. I know
where they've been by the wrinkles and creases
of a hot night's sleep, by what's left
in the bathwater when I rise steaming and clean.

SISTER MARY APPASSIONATA RECOUNTS
A FOLKTALE

No, no, no, no she said, squirming
beneath the convertible top
of the '57 Chevy, hemmed in
by his more experienced words,
defter hands. Out in the night
the brooding, drooling one-handed
danger the radio said had just escaped
stalked them both, but he was breathing
too loud for her to hear. *I'm*
saving myself. Take your hands
away. Take me home now please.
He did, the ache of teenage love denied
nearly doubling him over the wheel
each time he had to clutch or brake.
They found her father robed on his lawn,
hands on hips like some angry god,
enraged over rainbow bruises
on his little girl's throat,
the wrinkled skirt and angora sweater,
stains of mortal passion on his pants
and, just above where she sat, stuck
in the car's rag top, time's
glittering awful weapon lovely and lethal
as a scythe, the hook.

SISTER MARY APPASSIONATA LECTURES
THE FOLKLORE CLASS:
DOCTRINES OF THE STRAWBERRY

Mary, full of the mercy only
mothers know, hides the souls
of unchristened infants, guilty
as sure as they're born, in seeds
of strawberries, Jesus' favorite fruit,
and when He's picked and had His fill,
walking out into heaven's
misty meadows and groves weeping over
the gross appetites of the wicked,
thinness of the good, and after
nature's run its course, their beauty
passing through Him like too much
of any good thing, the seeds are left
to be covered with the dirt of paradise,
time's never ceasing tide, but soon
to rise again in blossoms of white flower
and plump red fruit, bitter and sweet
as blood, as life,
waiting for Him to come again.

SISTER MARY APPASSIONATA LECTURES
THE EIGHTH GRADE BOYS AND GIRLS
ON THE THINGS OF THIS WORLD,
THE THINGS OF THE OTHER

1.
God's at the bottom of the Sea of Japan,
a giant catfish old as darkness, slumbering
in fecund ooze, compost of creation, slimy
as liver. He dreams the world. Each twitch

of His whiskers, fins and tail means
another city leveled, another ten thousand
in over their heads. Civilizations go
to sleep each night praying God won't stir

or flop, make waves; won't, raging, rise.

2.
In every sudden winter river, God's what
hardens, that beast and man might stiffly
walk or glide across, a miracle,
each exhalation an aura, halo of holiness.

God's what sizzles the frying egg from clear
to white, garlic's spinning hiss, blight
that hastens falling fruit, earth's kiss dark
as a bruise, awful hardness that seizes

every lover, corpse, His sticky seed our dew.

3.
The Pharoah's personal physician was called
Shepherd of the Royal Anus, which goes
to show that sometimes gods move in
the commonest ways, words made flesh. Jesus

spat at blind men just to make them see.

4.
Rue cures the horniest witch's curse,
shrivels the lecher's stiff and massive passion.
Weasels and priests feed on its leaves
before going out to charm the snake.

Exorcists steep a leaf in blessed water

to tempt young girls from toadstools, scald
the throat of one possessed, sealing
the demon's blaspheming lips. In times of dread,
piles of smoldering dead, place it in church,

the baby's bed, near every mirror, fire,

it clears the head. Girls, put it where
your latest lover was, to draw out the ache
of generation. Life's a loss. Spend each day
adding, subtracting, recounting the expulsion

from the garden. Brew a cup of tears. And rue.

5.
The eyes shoot rays that photograph the world, no matter
how bad the composition, the light. Pius IX, good
and well meaning as they come, had the evil eye. He once
looked a baby out of its mother's arms high above Rome's
cobblestones and watched it plummet to earth, a fat,
ripe melon. When he blessed, walls went out of plumb,
mortar was changed back to water and sand, laborers fell
screaming from heaven, scaffolding collapsing like
cards. Ships and virgins went down like tons
of bricks. Only a greater gift can guard against
the evil eye. Mussolini kept his hands in his pants pockets
when Alphonso of Spain came to see him. He knew a handful
of the family jewels can soothe the wound of sight,
overcome the most glittering malice. If in the last six months
you've shed no tear, God will fill your eyes with cataracts.

Still today we veil widows and brides, spend our hard-earned
coins on the eyes of the dead. My own father died
of a broken heart because his mother stared at a picture
of the Sacred Heart on the bedroom wall as her husband labored
above her to plant the seed, her cries of love a prayer.
Because of the eyes everything connects.

6.
Love equals gravity. A net. Handful of ocean
your mother carried in her belly, and with
your father warmed over hearth's glowing coals
to brew you. You kicked, swam, grew fins

and tail, feet, visage and soul: love's phylogeny.

Mother's fingers, woven behind your skull
fragile as an egg, held you as she sang you awake.
Each word caught. Your lovers' sure hands
will unravel the web to spin you new. It all

gives way the day you fall all the way to age.

SISTER MARY APPASSIONATA LECTURES THE PRE-MED CLASS

1. A Lesson in Anatomy

500 million years ago Mother Eve
suffered a terrible blow from God's
left hand. The top of her spinal cord,
wriggling like a snake, swelled
into a brain the size of two apples.

The vagus nerve ties head to heart,
body to soul. The brain makes us
both angel and beast, cynic and believer,
its tortuous corridors are endless, tubing
to cool the furnace of the heart.

The body's a vertebrate, its skin
and sinew dressing barest bone, but
the head's a crustacean, bony shell
encompassing memory, idea and will,
sweet meat that lies inside, making us

wise as the sea. Without memory we'd
read the same story every day, never
chilling our pleasure by seeing
the beginning with the last things
in mind, love the very same lover

over and over the first time, wake
each dawn wonderful and eloquent as Adam.
The splintered teeth and shins of saints
endear them to us. Charred timbers
of the ancient room we were born into,

bones are most enduring.

2. *Figures of Love, Spending Our Lives*

Each cell's the image and likeness
of the wriggling, snake-tailed Adam
and the apple-sweet, blood-plump egg
of Eve who came together in a garden
of their love the day it all began.

An act of love plugs in the universe
again, strews eels, oysters and salmon
under the seas, toadstools and lilies,
rams and ewes over fields, portraits
of two parents on every bedroom's wall.

Onan the Canaanite? What a waste.
The figures of love are counted always
in twos, above and below, behind
or in front, recto, verso, in and out.
Love's the one heat of every race,

lover and beloved against the clock.
The Flood rose over us because it grew
too easy for women and men to love
themselves. Cursed be they who spend
their lives in puddles on the ground.

3. *The Four Fluids*

Chemistry informs us, quickens even
the dead. Four fluids God gave Adam
combine and recombine, gurgle
and roar, simmer and cool even as we do,
in the body's labyrinthine tubes.

Blood. Dark as well water when it
pools, deep enough to drown us all.
A race's history smeared thin as dust
over the pathologist's slide, life
inscribed, unfathomable as the tides.

Milk. Blood filtered by the loveliness
of breasts, kiss of aching nipples soft as
baby's breath, one of love's recurring
wounds, smooth as the belly rounded
and taut. In a frigid world, it's fire.

Tears. Blood conducted through canals
of sense: touch, sight, scents, listen
and sing. Juice fermented from fruit
of generation. It's how we pronounce
our sentence, mourn the receding sea.

Semen. Blood boiled, concentrated in
love's retort. Man's acrid dew. God's
manna brightening our fields even as we
sleep and love, live and breathe. Yeast
we rise by. Puddles of the sea that spawned us.

4. *Doctrines of the Breath*

Long as we live we just can't overtake
the heart, which, even when it's resting,
strokes four times faster than the lungs.

Life culminates in exhalation. The last one
bears the soul, which flies out whistling
like a dove to search for solid ground.

He's a fool who, all ears, spends his life
listening, knowing every breath could be
the last. Only to listen means too much

gets by. Shamans breathe so fast they learn
to fly and see all things. Slow respiration
means no passion. The deepest meditation, only

time we reach the peace each of us seeks,
a place of hibernation cold as bone or snow,
only time we're really holy, means

no breath at all.

5. *Bacteria and Weather, Treasure and Bones*

Our dead we give back to bacteria,
beetle, grub and worm, who carry them
back to the elements, earth, water,
fire and air, where they're born again
into feather and snail, desert flower,
moss and star-dew, mildew, fog and wind.

Their softest breathing becomes all
our weather. Their burrows and barrows
are our valleys, their mounds our hills.
Rivers carry them back to us, away.
What we build they bear the weight of.
Every well and foundation we dig

reapportions the treasure of their bones.

6. *The Nature of Love*

Because God couldn't figure how to be
everywhere He invented mothers. Women and men

are the only animals that drink when there's no
thirst, love in and out of season, recognize
the lineaments of God beneath a lover's clothes.
God made us pupils, gave us rods and cones so we

could really see. Billions have gone, millions
today are on the way because they can't know. Love.

The paramecium, which needs no other to work
its history, still seeks out others like
itself, powerless to couple yet groping, clumping
through life's utter night toward love. Every fossil

solves for us part of love's puzzle, stones
and bones that bore us all the way from sea and tree

to now. Lovers wind like strands of protein,
dance of the double helix, Eve and Adam every time
again. It wounds and heals, drum of heart's systole
and diastole, urgent peristalsis of flesh and soul.

7. The Nature of Vision

Look at a woman in that certain way
and you've already known her. (It was
a son looked on as a god who first saw

this.) Too much selfishness can drive
the young or old man blind, his eyes
clenched tightly as a fist. Because

we would not see, God grew mad enough
to spit, changed our dust to mud,
rubbed it on our eyes. Leonardo

saw that the artist's vision could
light the world. Hume showed us
we could look our Maker right in the eye.

No one's as wise or eloquent as the eye.
It knows seven million colors, every
variation of night and day. We've only

so many words. Every feature of the heart's
terrain grows visible to one whose
shortsightedness has been corrected for by

love. Fleeting omens of our incipient blindness,
every sneeze chills, stills the heart, on
every pair of eyes calls down the dark.

Age? The blossoming astigmatism, last
great cataract, evening racing over fields,
sea beneath the storm, the starless night.

8. *Last Things*

In the graveyard late at night, ear
to the ground, you can hear the dead
squeal, grunt like boar and sow, crackle
like fat dripping from the roasting spit

of time, burst like May seed pods,
speak your name in a parent's voice.
Most men slip into earth's hard sea
whispering their mother's name, most women

their father's. In death a woman bleeds
under each horned moon, a man stays hard
as on the wedding night, both of them
sweating as if in fever or love.

In three years the coffin explodes
from all the nails and hair, every body's
progeny. Death will come at you
like no other lover, whipping your face

with her long hair as she rides you
away, man, bony thighs gripping you
hard, her voice a storm tormenting
the pine-tops, plunging his icy hand

between your limbs, woman, teeth and tongue
lightly at your throat, whispering "It's never
felt this way before." Death's got
many lovers, no friends but the crow and fly.

Some soils keep you plump and firm
forever, others suck you dry in just one day.
The higher the clouds, the better you weather;
the deeper the grave, the better you keep.

SISTER MARY APPASSIONATA LECTURES
THE NEUROLOGY CLASS

If woman and man are willful, mindful hunks
of tissue, blood and bone, what is it wills, minds

them? If they're wills and minds embodied to make them
real enough to move to love what is it embodies them?

For two years Soviet scientists with stainless blades
sliced up Lenin's brain, yet learned nothing about

learning. Technicians splattered Walt Whitman's
brain on the laboratory floor and tried to claim

it was an accident. Is knowledge the last supper?
Worms learn tricks by feasting on worms who've already

learned. So do we cannibalize our past. The flash
of light erupting in the neural cell bright as

Venus rising or stars falling from heaven rescues us
from caves of skull, root and bark of limbs, blazes

into thought, a gift of fire, we think, we know.